THE TRUTH ABOUT HIPPOS

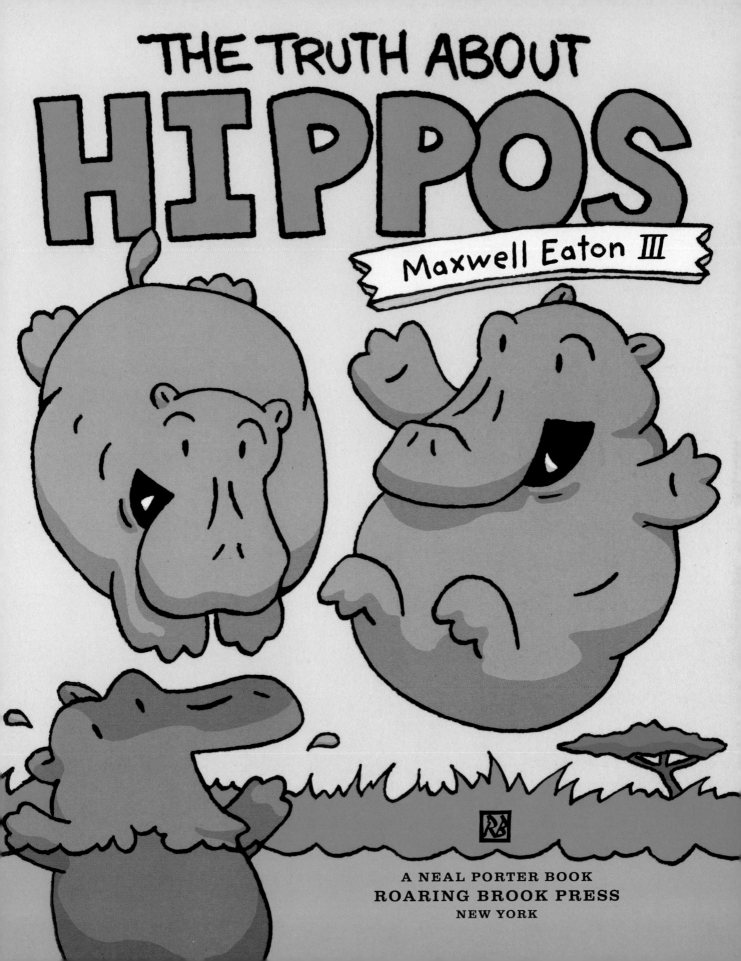

THE TRUTH ABOUT
HIPPOS

Maxwell Eaton III

A NEAL PORTER BOOK
ROARING BROOK PRESS
NEW YORK

FOR EEE

Copyright © 2018 by Maxwell Eaton III
A Neal Porter Book
Published by Roaring Brook Press
Roaring Brook Press is a division of Holtzbrinck
Publishing Holdings Limited Partnership
175 Fifth Avenue, New York, NY 10010
The art for this book was created using pen and ink with digital coloring.
mackids.com

ISBN: 978-1-62672-667-3
Library of Congress Control Number: 2017944677

Our books may be purchased in bulk for promotional, educational, or business use. Please
contact your local bookseller or the Macmillan Corporate and Premium Sales Department at
(800) 221-7945 ext. 5442 or by e-mail at MacmillanSpecialMarkets@macmillan.com.

First edition, 2018
Book design by Kristie Radwilowicz

Printed in China by Shaoguan Fortune Creative Industries Co. Ltd.,
Shaoguan, Guangdong Province

1 3 5 7 9 10 8 6 4 2

This is a hippopotamus.

There are two kinds of hippos:

and

PYGMY HIPPOS

(sounds like pig-mee)

A pygmy hippo can weigh the same as a large pig.

And a baby pygmy hippo is the size of a small dog.

Pygmy hippos like the muddy shores
of rivers and lakes in thick forests.

Common hippos mostly eat grass.

It's all there is around here.

HIPPOS USE THEIR TOUGH LIPS TO PLUCK GRASS AND NIBBLE. →

Pygmy hippos eat grass, leaves, fruits, and roots.

If a hippo sees someone it doesn't like, it opens its mouth to show off its razor-sharp teeth.

When a hippo goes to the bathroom, it flicks its tail back and forth, splattering everything that comes out!

Hippos can't actually swim.

HIPPOS ARE DENSER THAN WATER,
WHICH MEANS THEY SINK LIKE A ROCK.

Instead, they walk underwater or push off and sail through the water like otters.

Common hippos and pygmy hippos both spend their days resting.

HIPPOS ARE NOCTURNAL. THAT MEANS THEY SLEEP ALL DAY AND STAY UP ALL NIGHT.

Common hippos stay in the water in large groups.

Pygmy hippos relax in the shade all alone.

At night, both species of hippo leave the water to look for food. Pygmy hippos search the forest floor.

Common hippos will walk miles
by themselves to find enough grass.

But when morning comes, the hippos
head back home to rest, digest, and . . .

Hippos have big teeth, but that doesn't keep them completely safe.

Common hippos are threatened by hunting.

And pygmy hippos are losing their quiet forests.

But you can help by learning more about hippos and then teaching others.

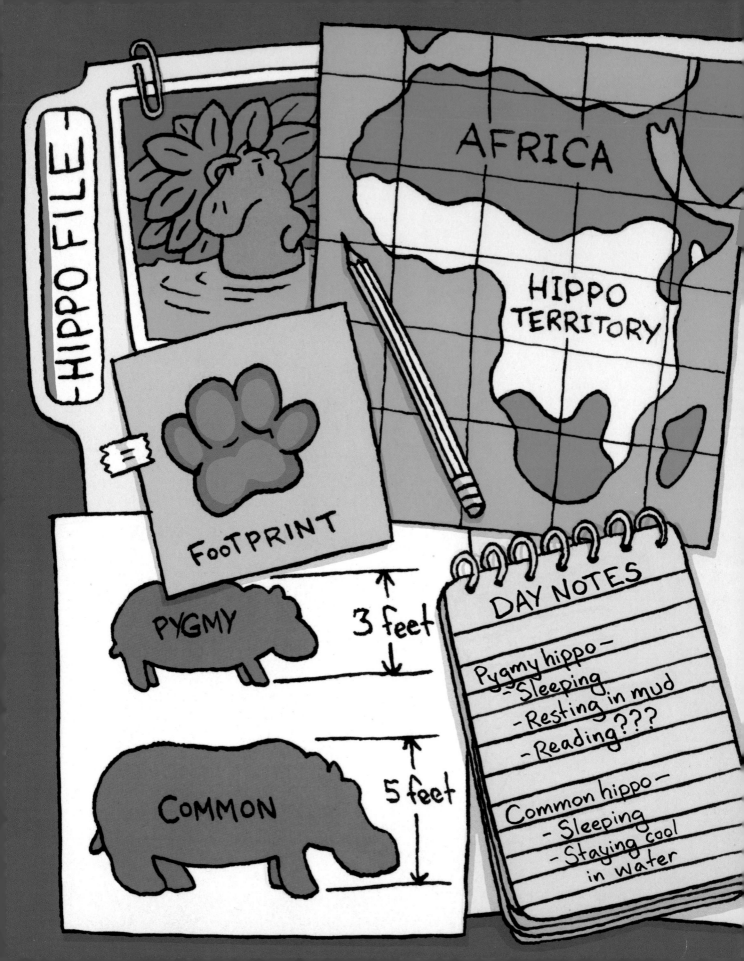

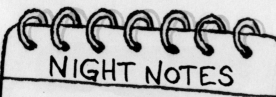

NIGHT NOTES

Pygmy hippo—
- Looking for food
- Eating fruit and leaves

Common hippo—
- Long walk to grass
- Eating grass
- Biking?!! (really bad)

WHAT??

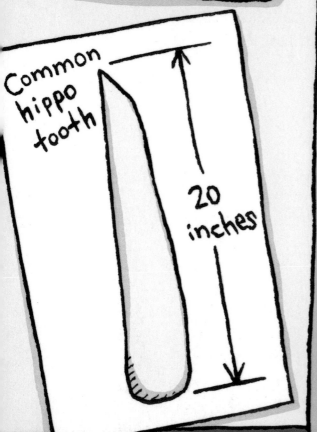

Common hippo tooth

20 inches

Further Research

BOOKS FOR PYGMY-SIZED HIPPOS

George and Martha, James Marshall, Houghton Mifflin, 1972.

Hippos, Glenn Feldhake, Colin Baxter Photography, 2005.

Hippos Are Huge!, Jonathan London, illustrated by Matthew Trueman, Candlewick Press, 2015.

BOOKS FOR COMMON-SIZED HIPPOS

The Behavior Guide to African Mammals, Richard Despard Estes, illustrated by Daniel Otte, University of California Press, 1991.

The Encyclopedia of Mammals, David Macdonald, ed., Facts on File, 2001.

The Hippos: Natural History and Conservation, S. K. Eltringham, Academic Press, 1999.

National Audubon Society Field Guide to African Wildlife, Peter C. Alden, Richard D. Estes, Duane Schlitter, Bunny McBride, Knopf, 1995.